CHRONICLES OF INDIAN STYLE

TRACING THE TRANSFORMATIONS OF TRADITIONAL AND CONTEMPORARY FASHION

DR. JAGADEESH PILLAI

|| Dedicated to all wisdom seekers around the World ||

୫

Contents

Contents

Prayer

**"Om Bhadram Karnebhih Shrunuyaama
DevaahBhadram Pashyemaakshabhiryajatraah
SthirairangaistushtuvaamsastanoobhihVyashema
Devahitam YadaayuhSwasti Na Indro
VridhashravaahSwasti Nah Pooshaa
VishwavedaahSwasti Nastaarkshyo ArishtanemihSwasti
No Brihaspatir DadhaatuOm Shantih, Shantih, Shantih"**

The literal meaning of this mantra is: OM. O Gods! Let us
hear auspicious words from our ears. O reverent Gods! Let
us behold propitious visions from our eyes, let our organs
and body be stable, healthy, and strong. Let us do that
which is pleasing to the gods in the life span allotted to us.
May Indra, inscribed in the scriptures, bring us fortune!
May Pushan, the knower of the world, grant us prosperity!
May Trakshya, who vanquishes enemies, bestow us with
blessings! May Brihaspati bring us success!
OM Peace, Peace, Peace.

About The Author

Dr. Jagadeesh Pillai is a renowned Guinness World Record holder, writer, and researcher hailing from Varanasi, also known as the abode of Lord Shiva. With a Ph.D. in Vedic Science and a range of creative ideas and achievements, he is a true polymath. He is the author of more than 100 books including Research Publications. Although his roots can be traced back to Kerala, the people of Varanasi hold him in high regard and affectionately consider him one of their own.

In 1998, Dr. Pillai was offered a job at Banaras Hindu University, but he left the position after only two months to pursue greater goals in life. He believed that in order to study Indian scriptures and engage in other creative endeavours, he needed to retire from the daily grind of working solely for money at a young age.

He started an export business from scratch, using the knowledge he had gained from a previous job in the industry. His intelligence and unique approach to business led to great success in a short period of time, earning him more in just a decade and a half than he would have in a lifetime working in a government job. Upon the passing of Dr. APJ Abdul Kalam, Dr. Pillai decided to leave the business and dedicate himself to reading, studying, researching, and experimenting.

During his tenure in the export business, Dr. Pillai traveled to over 16 countries, gaining valuable insight and experiencing the world and life in detail.

Dr. Pillai has achieved four Guinness World Records in the following subjects:

"Script to Screen" - In this record, Dr. Pillai produced and directed an animation film within the shortest time possible, breaking the previous record set by Canadians. He has also received numerous national and international awards and recognitions for this achievement.

Longest Line of Postcards - For this record, Dr. Pillai created a line of 16,300 postcards on the occasion of the 163rd anniversary of Indian Postal Day. The event also included a questionnaire about the Indian flag.

Largest Poster Awareness Campaign - Dr. Pillai designed an awareness campaign on the subject of "Beti Bachao - Beti Padhao" (Save the Girl Child - Educate the Girl Child) to achieve this record.

Largest Envelope - In tribute to the Indian Prime Minister's "Make in India" initiative, Dr. Pillai created a 4000 square meter envelope using waste paper to achieve this record.

Attempted - **70000 Candles on a 210 kg Cake** - To celebrate the 70th Indian Independence Day, Dr. Pillai attempted to light 70,000 candles on a 210 kg cake, which was recorded in World Records India.

Attempted - **Documentary on Dhamek Stupa of Sarnath in 17 Languages** - Dr. Pillai attempted to create a documentary on the Dhamek Stupa of Sarnath, dubbing it in 17 different languages. The result of this attempt is currently awaiting confirmation from the Guinness World Records.

Dr. Pillai is skilled in teaching the Bhagavad Gita, a Hindu scripture, and is popular among young people. He has helped many young people improve their lives through his motivational teachings.

In addition to teaching, he has composed and sung numerous Sanskrit Bhajans and patriotic songs.

He has also written and directed several short films and documentaries for awareness campaigns, and has volunteered with the police in both UP and Kerala to spread awareness about various issues through videos and photography.

Incredibly, he has produced and directed over 100 documentaries about the city of Varanasi, all on his own.

He has also helped and guided more than 25 boys and girls to achieve world records through creative and innovative methods. He is a multifaceted person who uses his intellect and the blessings given to him by God to excel in various areas. He is both a teacher and a student, always learning and teaching, and is able to master any subject he comes across.

He is a selfless social activist and motivational speaker who has overcome struggles and failures to become a successful and enthusiastic individual with a rich life experience.

In addition to his work with the Bhagavad Gita, he is also an efficient Tarot card reader, Astro-Vastu consultant, and a talented singer and composer. He has sung the entire Ram Charita Manas and Bhagavad Gita in his own compositions, and has sung the phrase "Lokah Samastha Sukhino Bhavantu" in 50 different languages. He is currently working on a detailed and scientific study of Vedas, Upanishads, Puranas, and the Bhagavad Gita. He has also composed and sung the Hanuman Chalisa and Gayatri Mantra in 108 and 1008 different compositions, respectively.

Awards - Four Times Guinness World Records, Winner of Mahatma Gandhi Vishwa Shanti Puraskar, Mahatma Gandhi Global Peace Ambassador, Kashi Ratna Award, Dr. APJ Abdul Kalam Motivational Person of the Year 2017, Mother Teresa Award, Indira Gandhi Priyadarshini Award, Bharat Vikas Ratna Award, Udyog Ratna Award, Vigyan Prasar Award, Poorvanchal Ratn Samman.

PREFACE

As an avid fashion enthusiast, I have been fascinated by the evolution and diversity of Indian fashion for many years. I have studied the history, culture, and artistic expression of Indian fashion with an enthusiasm that has only grown as I've observed more and more styles and trends. My goal for this book, The Indian Fashion: A Look into the Evolution and Diversity of Indian Traditional and Modern Fashion, is to share this enthusiasm with readers by providing an in-depth look at one of the most vibrant and influential fashion industries in the world.

This book is intended to serve as an introduction to the Indian fashion industry for readers who are new to the subject. It explores the evolution of Indian fashion from its traditional roots to the modern-day trends. The book covers various topics, including the development of different styles and trends, the emergence of popular fashion designers, and the impact of Bollywood on Indian fashion. It also examines the economics of the Indian fashion industry and explores how technological and societal changes have shaped its evolution.

The book draws on research from a variety of sources, including interviews with key figures in the Indian fashion industry, archival materials, and cultural analysis. I have also conducted extensive field research in India, including attending fashion shows, interviewing fashion designers, and visiting locations associated with the production of Indian fashion. Through this research, I hope to provide readers with a comprehensive understanding of the Indian fashion industry and its various components.

I am deeply passionate about the art of Indian fashion and hope that this book will help to spread the appreciation of this wonderful art form. I believe that Indian fashion has a great deal to offer to the world and I am excited to share its cultural and historical significance with my readers.

I

Introduction to Indian Fashion

India is a country renowned for its rich cultural heritage and diverse traditions. One aspect of this cultural richness is the diverse fashion styles that have evolved in India over the centuries. Indian fashion has a rich and storied history, with influences from various cultures, religions, and historical events shaping its evolution.

In this chapter, we will delve into the world of Indian fashion, exploring its origins, the different styles and influences that have shaped it, and the current state of fashion in India. We will examine both traditional Indian fashion and the modern adaptations that have emerged in recent years.

The Origin of Indian Fashion

The history of Indian fashion can be traced back to the

Indus Valley Civilization, where evidence of intricate clothing and jewelry have been found. As different cultures and religions invaded and settled in India, they brought with them their own unique styles and fashion practices, which merged with the existing local traditions to create a distinct style. For example, the Mughals introduced the concept of lavish embellishments, such as intricate embroidery, in their clothing, while the British colonial rule brought western styles and tailoring techniques to India.

Traditional Indian Fashion

Traditional Indian fashion is steeped in cultural and religious significance. It is an expression of identity, reflecting the values and beliefs of different communities in India. Different regions in India have their own unique traditional styles, with variations in fabrics, colors, and embellishments. Some of the most well-known traditional Indian styles include:

Sari: The sari is a long piece of cloth that is draped around the body and is considered one of the most traditional and iconic garments in India. It is usually made of cotton, silk, or other lightweight fabrics, and can be plain or heavily embellished. The style of draping the sari varies from region to region, with each style reflecting the cultural and social traditions of that area.

Kurta: The Kurta is a loose-fitting tunic that is worn by men and women in India. It is usually made of cotton or silk and is often embroidered or embellished with intricate designs. The Kurta is a versatile garment that can be worn with a range of other traditional Indian attire, such as churidar pants or lehenga skirts.

Lehnga: The Lehnga is a long skirt that is worn by women in India. It is often accompanied by a tight-fitting choli (blouse) and a dupatta (long scarf). The Lehnga is a popular garment for special occasions, such as weddings and festivals, and can be made of a range of fabrics, including silk, cotton, and georgette.

Dhoti: The Dhoti is a traditional Indian garment that is worn by men in India. It is a long piece of cloth that is draped around the waist and legs and is considered a symbol of Indian culture and tradition. The Dhoti is often worn with a Kurta or a Nehru jacket and is a popular garment for formal occasions.

Contemporary Indian Fashion

In recent years, Indian fashion has undergone a revolution, with designers experimenting with new materials, styles, and designs. Contemporary Indian fashion is a fusion of traditional styles and modern Western influences, and is characterized by bold colors, intricate embellishments, and unique silhouettes.

Designers in India are pushing the boundaries of traditional Indian fashion, creating modern adaptations of traditional garments and incorporating new materials, such as metallic fabrics and digital prints. Indian fashion has also gained international recognition, with Indian designers showcasing their collections at international fashion weeks and Indian fashion brands being sold in high-end department stores across the world.

Indian fashion is a rich and diverse field that has evolved over the centuries, reflecting the cultural, religious, and historical influences of the country. From traditional saris and kurtas to contemporary adaptations of traditional styles, Indian fashion is a testament to the creative spirit and cultural heritage of India. This chapter serves as an introduction to the fascinating world of Indian fashion, and the rest of the book will delve deeper into the transformations and innovations that have shaped this vibrant industry.

"Indian fashion is a reflection of our culture,
our diversity, and our values."

– Manish Mal.

☙

II

History of Indian Fashion

The history of Indian fashion is a rich and diverse tapestry that spans thousands of years. From the Indus Valley Civilization to the modern fashion industry of today, Indian fashion has been shaped by a multitude of cultural, religious, and historical influences. In this chapter, we will explore the key events and influences that have shaped the evolution of Indian fashion over the centuries.

The Indus Valley Civilization

The history of Indian fashion can be traced back to the Indus Valley Civilization, which flourished in the northwestern region of the Indian subcontinent around 2500 BCE. Excavations of the Indus Valley sites have uncovered evidence of intricate clothing and jewelry, suggesting that fashion was an important aspect of life in this ancient civilization. The clothing and jewelry found at

Indus Valley sites were made of cotton and gold, and were decorated with intricate designs and patterns.

The Vedic Period

The Vedic period, which lasted from 1500 BCE to 500 BCE, was a time of great religious and cultural significance in India. During this period, Hinduism, Buddhism, and Jainism emerged as major religions in India, and their teachings and rituals had a profound impact on the development of Indian fashion. During the Vedic period, clothing was used to distinguish different castes and professions, and was also a symbol of religious and cultural identity.

The Mughal Empire

The Mughal Empire, which ruled India from the 16th to the 19th century, had a profound impact on Indian fashion. The Mughals introduced the concept of lavish embellishments, such as intricate embroidery, in their clothing, and their influence can still be seen in traditional Indian fashion today. The Mughals also brought with them their own unique fashion styles, which merged with existing local styles to create a distinct Mughal style of fashion.

The British Colonial Period

The British colonial rule in India, which lasted from the late 18th century to the mid-20th century, brought Western styles and tailoring techniques to India. The British introduced new fabrics, such as silk and cotton, and the use of the sewing machine, which revolutionized the Indian fashion industry. The British also influenced Indian fashion by imposing strict dress codes for different social classes, which helped to establish a more formal and structured approach to fashion in India.

Independence and the Modern Era

The independence of India from British rule in 1947 marked a new era in the history of Indian fashion. The country was eager to embrace its own cultural heritage and traditions, and fashion played a key role in this cultural resurgence. Indian designers and fashion houses began to experiment with traditional styles and materials, incorporating new ideas and techniques to create modern adaptations of traditional Indian fashion.

In recent years, Indian fashion has gained international recognition, with Indian designers showcasing their collections at international fashion weeks and Indian fashion brands being sold in high-end department stores across the world. The Indian fashion industry is now a thriving sector, employing thousands of people and generating billions of dollars in revenue each year.

The history of Indian fashion is a rich and diverse tapestry that reflects the cultural, religious, and historical influences of the country. From the Indus Valley Civilization to the modern fashion industry of today, Indian fashion has evolved and transformed over the centuries, reflecting the creative spirit and cultural heritage of India. This chapter provides a comprehensive overview of the key events and influences that have shaped the history of Indian fashion, and serves as a foundation for exploring the transformations and innovations that have shaped this vibrant industry.

ಚ

"Fashion is a reflection of the times, and
Indian fashion is no exception - it has evolved
and diversified over the centuries."

III

Traditional Indian Textiles and Garments

Traditional Indian textiles and garments are an integral part of the country's rich cultural heritage and are renowned for their intricate designs, rich colors, and luxurious fabrics. From the hand-woven silks of Varanasi to the colorful bandhani prints of Rajasthan, traditional Indian textiles and garments are a celebration of the country's artistic and cultural traditions. In this chapter, we will explore the key traditional Indian textiles and garments, and examine their cultural significance and role in the evolution of Indian fashion.

Hand-Woven Silks

Hand-woven silks are among the most luxurious and sought-after traditional Indian textiles. The most famous hand-woven silks come from the city of Varanasi, located in the northern state of Uttar Pradesh. The silks produced in Varanasi are known for their rich colors, soft texture, and intricate designs, which are created using a variety of techniques, including Ikat, Bandhini, and Brocade.

Cotton Fabrics

Cotton is a staple fabric in India, and is widely used for both formal and informal garments. Indian cotton fabrics are renowned for their breathable and comfortable qualities, and are often decorated with intricate designs, such as block prints and embroidery. Some of the most famous cotton fabrics produced in India include Chikankari from Lucknow, Madras checks from Chennai, and Kota Doria from Rajasthan.

Traditional Garments

Traditional Indian garments are diverse and reflect the cultural heritage of the different regions of the country. Some of the most famous traditional garments include the Sari, the Salwar Kameez, the Lehenga Choli, and the Kurta Pyjama.

The Sari is a long piece of cloth that is wrapped around the body and is the most iconic traditional garment in India. Saris are made from a variety of fabrics, including silk, cotton, and georgette, and are available in a range of colors, designs, and styles. The Sari is an integral part of Indian culture and is widely worn on special occasions and celebrations.

The Salwar Kameez is a loose-fitting garment that consists of a tunic top, called a Kameez, and loose pants, called a Salwar. This garment is popular in northern India and is available in a range of styles and designs, from traditional to contemporary.

The Lehenga Choli is a traditional garment that originated in northern India and is now widely worn throughout the country. The Lehenga Choli consists of a long skirt, a short blouse, and a dupatta, or scarf. The Lehenga Choli is often decorated with intricate designs and is available in a range of styles and designs, from traditional to modern.

The Kurta Pyjama is a traditional Indian outfit that consists of a long, loose tunic top, called a Kurta, and loose pants, called Pyjamas. The Kurta Pyjama is popular in northern India and is available in a range of styles and designs, from traditional to contemporary.

Traditional Indian textiles and garments are an integral part of the country's rich cultural heritage and are renowned for their intricate designs, rich colors, and luxurious fabrics. From hand-woven silks to cotton fabrics, traditional Indian textiles and garments are a celebration of the country's artistic and cultural traditions. This chapter provides a comprehensive overview of the key traditional Indian textiles and garments, and examines their cultural significance and role in the evolution of Indian fashion.

"The beauty of Indian fashion lies in its ability to blend traditional and modern styles to create something unique and timeless."

਍

IV

Evolving Styles and Trends in Indian Fashion

Evolving Styles and Trends in Indian Fashion

Indian fashion has undergone a major transformation over the last few decades, as the country has embraced contemporary styles and trends while still maintaining its rich cultural heritage. In this chapter, we will explore the evolution of Indian fashion and examine the key styles and trends that have emerged in recent years.

Influence of Western Fashion

One of the major drivers of change in Indian fashion has been the influence of Western fashion. Over the last few decades, Indian designers have been inspired by Western styles and have incorporated these into their designs, creating a unique fusion of traditional and contemporary styles. From the use of modern materials and silhouettes to the incorporation of Western patterns and prints, Indian fashion has been transformed by the influence of Western fashion.

Emergence of Bollywood Fashion

Another major influence on Indian fashion has been the rise of Bollywood, the Hindi-language film industry based in Mumbai. Bollywood has been instrumental in promoting Indian fashion and has helped to popularize traditional styles, such as the Sari, and contemporary styles, such as the Salwar Kameez. Bollywood celebrities have become style icons, and their fashion choices have had a significant impact on the Indian fashion industry.

Rise of Designer Labels

In recent years, the Indian fashion industry has seen the rise of numerous designer labels, which have helped to promote and elevate Indian fashion to new heights. From the traditional hand-woven silks of Varanasi to the contemporary designs of Mumbai and Delhi, Indian designer labels are producing a range of styles and designs that are capturing the attention of the world.

Key Styles and Trends

One of the key styles in Indian fashion today is the fusion of traditional and contemporary styles. This style blends traditional Indian textiles and patterns with contemporary silhouettes, materials, and embellishments to create a unique and modern look.

Another key trend in Indian fashion is the use of bold and bright colors, which are often inspired by the country's rich cultural heritage. From the vibrant hues of the Holi festival to the deep, rich colors of traditional Indian textiles, Indian fashion is characterized by its use of bold and bright colors.

The use of hand-crafted and traditional techniques, such as embroidery, printing, and weaving, is another key trend in Indian fashion. These techniques are often used to create unique and intricate designs that are not possible with modern methods, and they serve to celebrate the country's rich cultural heritage.

Indian fashion has undergone a major transformation over the last few decades, as the country has embraced contemporary styles and trends while still maintaining its rich cultural heritage. From the influence of Western fashion and the rise of Bollywood, to the emergence of designer labels and the popularity of fusion styles, Indian fashion is constantly evolving and adapting to new trends and styles. This chapter provides an overview of the key styles and trends that have emerged in recent years, and examines the role of tradition and culture in the evolution of Indian fashion.

"The evolution of Indian fashion is a
testament to the creativity and ingenuity of
its people."

∞

V
Diversity of Indian Clothing

India is a country of rich cultural diversity, and this diversity is reflected in the clothing worn by its people. From the traditional hand-woven silks of Varanasi to the contemporary styles of Mumbai and Delhi, Indian clothing is characterized by its rich heritage and unique aesthetic. In this chapter, we will examine the diversity of Indian clothing, and explore the key traditional and contemporary styles that are worn throughout the country.

Traditional Indian Clothing

India has a rich tradition of clothing, and each region of the country has its own unique styles and textiles. Some of the most iconic traditional Indian clothing styles include the Sari, the Salwar Kameez, and the Kurta. These styles are characterized by their use of traditional textiles, such as silk, cotton, and chiffon, and by the intricate embellishments and hand-crafted techniques that are used to create them.

Sari

The Sari is one of the most iconic traditional Indian clothing styles, and it is worn by women throughout the country. The Sari is a long piece of cloth, typically made of silk or cotton, that is draped around the body in a specific manner. It is often decorated with intricate embroidery, and it is considered to be a symbol of elegance and grace.

Salwar Kameez

The Salwar Kameez is a traditional Indian clothing style that is popular in northern India. It consists of a long tunic, called a Kurta, and loose pants, called Salwar, that are worn together. The Salwar Kameez is typically made of cotton or silk, and it is often decorated with intricate embroidery or printing.

Kurta

The Kurta is a traditional Indian tunic that is worn by both men and women. It is typically made of cotton or silk, and it is characterized by its long, loose silhouette. The Kurta is often worn with loose pants, such as the Salwar, and it is considered to be a symbol of simplicity and comfort.

Contemporary Indian Clothing

In recent years, the Indian fashion industry has embraced contemporary styles and trends, and this is reflected in the clothing that is worn by people throughout the country. From the fusion of traditional and contemporary styles to the rise of designer labels, Indian fashion is constantly evolving and adapting to new trends and styles.

Fusion Styles

One of the key styles in Indian fashion today is the fusion of traditional and contemporary styles. This style blends traditional Indian textiles and patterns with contemporary silhouettes, materials, and embellishments to create a unique and modern look.

Designer Labels

The rise of designer labels in India has helped to promote and elevate Indian fashion to new heights. From the traditional hand-woven silks of Varanasi to the contemporary designs of Mumbai and Delhi, Indian designer labels are producing a range of styles and designs that are capturing the attention of the world.

Indian clothing is characterized by its rich heritage and diverse styles. From the iconic Sari to the contemporary fusion styles, Indian clothing reflects the country's rich cultural diversity and its constant evolution and adaptation to new trends and styles. This chapter provides an overview of the key traditional and contemporary styles that are worn throughout India, and examines the diversity of Indian clothing and the role of tradition and culture in its evolution.

ಙ

"Indian fashion is a reflection of the country's rich cultural heritage, with each region having its own unique style."

༄

VI

Traditional Indian Embroidery and Accessories

Indian clothing is known for its intricate and ornate embellishments, and traditional Indian embroidery and accessories play a key role in this aesthetic. From the delicate hand-embroidered silks of Varanasi to the bold and colorful prints of Rajasthan, traditional Indian embroidery and accessories add a touch of elegance and richness to any outfit. In this chapter, we will examine the key traditional Indian embroidery styles and accessories, and explore the cultural and historical significance of these embellishments.

Traditional Indian Embroidery Styles

India has a rich tradition of embroidery, and each region of the country has its own unique styles and techniques. Some of the most iconic traditional Indian embroidery styles include:

Zari Work: Zari work is a type of embroidery that uses gold or silver threads to create intricate designs and patterns. It is often used on traditional Indian clothing, such as the Sari and the Kurta, and it is considered to be a symbol of wealth and elegance.

Kantha: Kantha is a type of hand-stitched embroidery that is popular in Bengal. It is characterized by its use of simple running stitches and bold, colorful designs, and it is often used to create vibrant and eye-catching textiles.

Phulkari: Phulkari is a type of embroidery that is popular in Punjab. It is characterized by its bold, colorful designs and its use of simple stitches, and it is often used to create vibrant and eye-catching textiles and clothing.

Chikankari: Chikankari is a type of hand-embroidery that is popular in Lucknow. It is characterized by its intricate and delicate designs, and it is often used to embellish traditional Indian clothing, such as the Sari and the Kurta.

Traditional Indian Accessories

In addition to traditional Indian embroidery, accessories also play a key role in the country's rich cultural heritage. From jewelry to handbags, traditional Indian accessories are characterized by their ornate designs, intricate embellishments, and cultural significance. Some of the most iconic traditional Indian accessories include:

Jhumka Earrings: Jhumka earrings are a type of traditional Indian earring that are characterized by their large, bell-shaped design. They are often embellished with intricate details and they are considered to be a symbol of traditional Indian elegance.

Nose Rings: Nose rings are a traditional Indian accessory that are worn by women throughout the country. They are often embellished with intricate designs and they are considered to be a symbol of cultural heritage and elegance.

Bindi: The Bindi is a small dot that is worn on the forehead by women in India. It is often embellished with intricate designs and it is considered to be a symbol of traditional Indian beauty and elegance.

Traditional Indian embroidery and accessories play a key role in the country's rich cultural heritage and aesthetic. From the intricate Zari work of Varanasi to the bold and colorful prints of Rajasthan, these embellishments add a touch of elegance and richness to any outfit. This chapter provides an overview of the key traditional Indian embroidery styles and accessories, and examines the cultural and historical significance of these embellishments. Whether worn for special occasions or as a daily statement, traditional Indian embroidery and accessories are an integral part of the country's cultural and fashion heritage.

"Indian fashion is a kaleidoscope of vibrant colors, intricate designs, and exquisite fabrics."

⁜

VII

Bollywood and Indian Fashion

Bollywood, India's film industry, has long been a major influence on Indian fashion. From the glamorous outfits worn by Bollywood stars to the iconic fashion moments depicted in films, Bollywood has shaped the way that Indian fashion is perceived both in India and abroad. In this chapter, we will examine the relationship between Bollywood and Indian fashion, and explore how this dynamic partnership has helped to shape and transform Indian fashion over the years.

Bollywood and Traditional Indian Fashion

For many years, Bollywood films have portrayed traditional Indian fashion in a romantic and nostalgic light, showcasing the beauty and elegance of traditional Indian textiles and garments. From saris to lehengas, these films have helped to keep traditional Indian fashion alive and relevant, even as the world around them has changed. Bollywood has also played a role in promoting traditional Indian crafts and techniques, such as hand-embroidery and block printing, by showcasing these skills in films and through the work of costume designers.

Bollywood and Modern Indian Fashion

In recent years, Bollywood has also played a key role in shaping the evolution of modern Indian fashion. Bollywood stars are often seen wearing the latest fashion trends, both on and off the big screen, and these trends are eagerly followed by fans around the world. From streetwear to couture, Bollywood has helped to bring a new level of sophistication and modernity to Indian fashion, and has helped to establish India as a major player in the global fashion industry.

Bollywood and the Fashion Industry

The relationship between Bollywood and the fashion industry is a dynamic one, with each influencing the other in different ways. On one hand, Bollywood provides a platform for fashion designers to showcase their work, through the costumes and outfits worn by stars in films. On the other hand, fashion designers often draw inspiration from Bollywood films and the latest trends, incorporating these styles into their own collections. This mutually beneficial partnership has helped to bring Indian fashion to a new level of visibility and popularity, both in India and abroad.

Bollywood and Indian fashion have a long and intertwined

history, with each influencing the other in different ways. From the romantic depictions of traditional Indian fashion in films, to the latest fashion trends showcased by Bollywood stars, this dynamic partnership has helped to shape and transform Indian fashion over the years. Whether through the costumes and outfits in films, or the work of designers inspired by Bollywood trends, Bollywood continues to play a major role in the development and evolution of Indian fashion.

"Indian fashion is a beautiful blend of the old and the new, creating a look that is both classic and contemporary."

⚭

VIII
Modern Indian Fashion Designers

In recent decades, India has experienced a boom in its fashion industry, with a growing number of talented and innovative designers emerging on the global stage. From couture houses to streetwear labels, these designers are drawing on the rich cultural heritage of India, as well as the latest global fashion trends, to create a unique and contemporary take on Indian fashion. In this chapter, we will examine the key modern Indian fashion designers, and explore their influence on the Indian fashion industry.

Manish Arora

Manish Arora is one of India's most renowned fashion designers, and he is known for his bold and colorful designs that draw on India's rich cultural heritage. Arora's work is characterized by its use of bright colors, intricate embroideries, and bold patterns, and he has become one of

India's most sought-after fashion designers, both in India and abroad.

Sabyasachi Mukherjee

Sabyasachi Mukherjee is a leading Indian fashion designer, who has made a name for himself with his luxurious and intricate designs. Mukherjee's work is characterized by its use of traditional Indian techniques, such as hand-embroidery and Zari work, and he is known for his elegant and sophisticated style.

Tarun Tahiliani

Tarun Tahiliani is a leading Indian fashion designer, who is known for his innovative and cutting-edge designs. Tahiliani's work is characterized by its use of luxurious materials, such as silks and velvets, and he is known for his ability to blend traditional Indian techniques with contemporary styles.

Ritu Kumar

Ritu Kumar is one of India's most established fashion designers, and she is known for her elegant and timeless designs. Kumar's work is characterized by its use of traditional Indian techniques, such as hand-embroidery and block printing, and she is known for her ability to create modern and stylish clothing that is rooted in India's rich cultural heritage.

Anamika Khanna

Anamika Khanna is a leading Indian fashion designer, who is known for her innovative and modern designs. Khanna's work is characterized by its use of bright colors and bold patterns, and she is known for her ability to blend traditional Indian techniques with contemporary styles.

India has a growing and thriving fashion industry, with a number of talented and innovative designers emerging on the global stage. From Manish Arora's bold and colorful designs to Sabyasachi Mukherjee's luxurious and intricate pieces, these designers are drawing on the rich cultural heritage of India, as well as the latest global fashion trends, to create a unique and contemporary take on Indian fashion. Whether they are working in couture houses or streetwear labels, these designers are helping to shape the future of the Indian fashion industry, and they are inspiring a new generation of designers to follow in their footsteps.

"Indian fashion is a celebration of culture,
art, and history, all rolled into one."

સ્ર

IX

The Impact of Indian Fashion on Society

Fashion is not just a matter of aesthetic appeal, it reflects the cultural and social values of a society. In India, fashion has been an integral part of the social and cultural fabric for centuries, influencing and being influenced by the changes in the society. This chapter explores the impact that Indian fashion has had on the society, and how it has evolved over time to keep pace with the changing times.

The influence of religion on Indian fashion

Religion has been a major influence on Indian fashion since ancient times. The traditional attire of Hindu women, for instance, has been influenced by the dress codes prescribed in the Hindu scriptures. Sarees and lehengas have been worn by women as a symbol of their devotion and to showcase their beauty. Similarly, the traditional attire of Muslim women, such as the burqa and the hijab, reflects their religious beliefs and customs.

The impact of colonialism on Indian fashion

The arrival of the British in India in the 18th century had a profound impact on Indian fashion. The British introduced western styles of clothing, which were adopted by the Indian aristocracy. This led to a fusion of western and Indian styles, giving birth to the Indo-Western fusion trend that is still popular today. The British also introduced new fabrics, such as muslin and calico, which were incorporated into traditional Indian garments, adding a new dimension to Indian fashion.

The influence of Bollywood on Indian fashion

Bollywood, the Hindi film industry, has been a major influence on Indian fashion since the 1920s. The glamorous and elaborate costumes worn by the actors have been a source of inspiration for Indian women. Bollywood has popularized a range of styles, from the traditional saree to the modern Western attire, influencing the fashion choices of millions of people across the country. The costumes worn in Bollywood films have also become a symbol of Indian culture and have been showcased at fashion events across the world.

The impact of Indian fashion on the economy

Indian fashion has had a significant impact on the economy. The fashion industry in India is estimated to be worth over \$40 billion, and is growing at a rapid pace. The industry employs millions of people, providing livelihoods and contributing to the growth of the economy. The exports of Indian fashion products have also increased, with India becoming one of the largest exporters of textiles and garments in the world.

The impact of Indian fashion on the environment

Fashion has also had an impact on the environment, with the production of fast fashion leading to a significant amount of waste and pollution. In India, traditional handloom and craft-based textiles are more sustainable, as they are made from natural fibers and produced using traditional techniques that are less harmful to the environment. These traditional textiles have been recognized as a cultural heritage and have been given the status of a geographical indication, which helps to protect and preserve the knowledge, skills and traditions associated with these textiles. Moreover, the use of natural fibers and dyes helps to reduce the environmental footprint of the fashion industry, and the use of sustainable practices can help to reduce the waste generated by the industry.

The impact of Indian fashion on women's empowerment

Indian fashion has also played a role in women's empowerment, especially in rural areas where the fashion industry provides livelihoods to millions of women. The fashion industry has provided women with opportunities to earn a living, develop their skills and become self-sufficient. The traditional handicrafts and textiles industry has also helped to preserve the cultural heritage of India, and the revival of these crafts has provided employment opportunities to many women. In addition, Indian fashion has also played a role in promoting gender equality, as more women are entering the fashion industry as designers, models and entrepreneurs.

Indian fashion has had a profound impact on the society, influencing the cultural and social values, the economy, the environment and women's empowerment. The fashion industry in India has grown and evolved over the years, reflecting the changing times and the changing needs of the society. From the traditional handloom textiles to the modern fashion designers, Indian fashion continues to reflect the diversity and richness of the country's culture and heritage. The impact of Indian fashion on the society highlights the importance of fashion as a cultural expression and a tool for social change.

"The diversity of Indian fashion is a testament to the country's vibrant and ever-changing culture."

୫ଓ

The Economics of Indian Fashion

The fashion industry is a major contributor to the Indian economy, and has grown rapidly in recent years. From traditional textiles and garments to modern fashion design, the economics of Indian fashion are complex and multifaceted. In this chapter, we will explore the different aspects of the economics of Indian fashion, and how they contribute to the growth and development of this vibrant and diverse industry.

Traditional Indian Textile and Garment Production

The production of traditional Indian textiles and garments is an important aspect of the Indian fashion industry, and employs a significant number of workers. From hand-loom weavers to embroidery artisans, these workers are the backbone of the traditional fashion industry, and help to keep traditional techniques and skills alive. The production of traditional textiles and garments is often centered in rural areas, and provides a source of income for many families.

The rise of modern Indian fashion

In recent years, the Indian fashion industry has experienced significant growth, driven by the rise of modern Indian fashion. From fashion designers to fashion retail, the modern fashion industry is centered in India's cities, and provides a major source of employment and income. This growth has been driven by a number of factors, including the increasing popularity of Indian fashion both in India and abroad, and the rise of a new generation of Indian fashion designers who are pushing the boundaries of traditional Indian fashion.

Export of Indian Fashion

The export of Indian fashion is another important aspect of the Indian fashion industry, and helps to bring Indian fashion to a global audience. From saris to modern fashion design, Indian fashion is in demand around the world, and the export of these products helps to contribute to the growth and development of the Indian fashion industry. Indian fashion is exported to a number of countries, including the United States, the United Kingdom, and the Middle East, and is often recognized for its high quality and unique style.

The Role of the Government

The government plays an important role in the

development of the Indian fashion industry, through policies and initiatives aimed at supporting the growth and development of the industry. From providing financial support to fashion designers to promoting Indian fashion abroad, the government has helped to create a supportive environment for the growth of the Indian fashion industry. The government has also implemented policies aimed at protecting traditional Indian textile and garment production, and promoting the use of sustainable materials and production methods.

The economics of Indian fashion are complex and multifaceted, encompassing traditional textile and garment production, the rise of modern Indian fashion, and the export of Indian fashion. The industry is a major contributor to the Indian economy, providing employment and income for many workers and helping to promote India's rich cultural heritage to a global audience. The government plays an important role in the development of the industry, through policies and initiatives aimed at supporting the growth and development of the Indian fashion industry. Whether through the production of traditional textiles and garments, the rise of modern Indian fashion, or the export of Indian fashion, the economics of Indian fashion are an important part of India's cultural and economic heritage, and will continue to play a major role in shaping the future of Indian fashion.

"Indian fashion is a celebration of the beauty
and diversity of the Indian people."

౮

XI

The Future of Indian Fashion

As the world continues to change and evolve, so does the fashion industry. The future of Indian fashion is shaped by various factors including innovation, sustainability, and globalization. In this chapter, we will explore these three key elements and how they are shaping the future of Indian fashion.

Innovation

Innovation is one of the key drivers of the fashion industry, and it is no different in India. The future of Indian fashion is being shaped by the use of new technologies, materials, and techniques. For example, the use of digital technologies such as 3D printing, virtual reality and augmented reality is changing the way in which fashion is designed, produced and consumed. These technologies are enabling designers to create unique and innovative designs that can be customized to the individual needs of consumers.

In addition, the use of sustainable and eco-friendly materials is also driving innovation in Indian fashion. This includes the use of natural fibers such as cotton, silk, and wool, as well as recycled and biodegradable materials. The use of these materials is helping to reduce the environmental impact of the fashion industry and to create more sustainable and eco-friendly fashion products.

Sustainability

Sustainability is becoming increasingly important in the fashion industry, and it is shaping the future of Indian fashion. The growing awareness of environmental issues, such as climate change and pollution, is driving consumers to demand more sustainable and environmentally friendly fashion products. In response to this demand, the fashion industry in India is focusing on sustainable practices such as reducing waste, using eco-friendly materials and reducing energy consumption.

The use of sustainable and eco-friendly materials, such as organic cotton and recycled polyester, is becoming more widespread in the Indian fashion industry. Moreover, many fashion designers and brands are working to reduce their carbon footprint by using renewable energy sources, reducing water usage and implementing sustainable production processes.

Globalization

The globalization of the fashion industry is having a

significant impact on the future of Indian fashion. The increasing internationalization of the fashion industry has led to a growing demand for Indian fashion products in international markets. This has led to the growth of the Indian fashion export industry, which is providing new opportunities for Indian fashion designers and brands.

Moreover, the globalization of the fashion industry is also increasing the exposure of Indian fashion to new cultures and trends. This is leading to the fusion of Indian and international styles, creating a new and unique form of fashion that reflects the diversity of Indian culture.

The future of Indian fashion is shaped by innovation, sustainability and globalization. These factors are driving the growth of the fashion industry in India, creating new opportunities for Indian fashion designers and brands. The future of Indian fashion is characterized by the use of sustainable and eco-friendly materials, the adoption of innovative technologies and the increasing internationalization of the industry. By embracing these changes, Indian fashion has the potential to become a leader in sustainable and innovative fashion and to continue to reflect the rich cultural heritage and diversity of India.

"Indian fashion is a reflection of the country's rich history and culture, and its evolution is a testament to its creativity and innovation."

☙

Other Books Of The Author

1. The Moments When I Met God
2. Kashiyile Theertha Pathangal
3. GURU GYAN VANI
4. Abhiprerak Gita
5. ASSI SE JAIN GHAT TAK
6. Hopelessness of Arjuna
7. The Soul and It's True Nature
8. Sense of Action (Karma)
9. Action through Wisdom
10. Action through Wisdom
11. THEORY AND PRACTICAL OF EVERY ACTION
12. LOGICAL UNDERSTANDING OF THE SUPREME
13. THE IMPERISHABLE SUPREME
14. Yatra Nishadraj se Hanuman Ghat Tak
15. Yatra Karnatak Ghat se Raja Ghat Tak
16. Yatra Pandey Ghat se Prayagraj Ghat Tak
17. Yatra Ranjendra Prasad Ghat se Dattatreya Ghat Tak
18. YaatraSindhiya Ghat se Gwaliar Ghat Tak
19. Yatra Mangala Gauri Ghat se Hanuman Gadhi Ghat Tak
20. Yatra Gaay Ghat Se Nishad Ghat Tak
21. MAA GANGA, GHATEN EVM UTSAV
22. Ganga Arti Dev Deepavali evam Any Utsav
23. Potentials of Digitalized India
24. VEDIC CONSCIOUSNESS
25. A Brief Introduction to Vedic Science
26. Kashi ke Barah Jyotirling
27. IMPACT OF MOTIVATION
28. Let's have a Milky Way Journey
29. Color Therapy in a Nutshell

ॐ

CONTACT

DR. JAGADEESH PILLAI

MBA & PhD in Vedic Science

Four Times Guinness World Record Holder

Winner of Mahatma Gandhi Vishwa Shanti Puraskar and
Global Peace Ambassador

Gemology, Astro & Vastu Consultant - Spiritual Counselor

Consultant for designing World Record Ideas

Efficient Tarot Card Reader

9839093003

myrichindia@gmail.com

drjagadeeshpillai@facebook

drjagadeeshpillai@instagram
jagadeeshpillai@youtube

www. JAGADEESHPILLAI.com

|| LOKAHA SAMASTHAHA SUKHINO BHAVANTU ||

• 75 •